Tell Me about the Presidents

Also by Mike Henry

Black History: More than Just a Month

What They Didn't Teach You in American History Class

What They Didn't Teach You in American History Class: The Second Encounter (Second Edition)

Tell Me about the Presidents

Lessons for Today's Kids from America's Leaders

Mike Henry

ROWMAN & LITTLEFIELD
Lanham • Boulder • New York • London

Published by Rowman & Littlefield
A wholly owned subsidiary of The Rowman & Littlefield Publishing Group, Inc.
4501 Forbes Boulevard, Suite 200, Lanham, Maryland 20706
www.rowman.com

Unit A, Whitacre Mews, 26-34 Stannary Street, London SE11 4AB

British Library Cataloguing in Publication Information Available

Library of Congress Cataloging-in-Publication Data

Henry, Mike, 1952-
  Tell me about the presidents : lessons for today's kids from America's leaders / Mike Henry.
     pages cm
  Includes bibliographical references.
  ISBN 978-1-4758-1703-4 (hardcover) — ISBN 978-1-4758-1704-1 (pbk.) — ISBN 978-1-4758-1705-8 (e-book) 1. Presidents—United States—Biography—Juvenile literature. 2. Presidents—United States—Miscellanea—Juvenile literature. I. Title.
  E176.1.H454 2015
  973.09'9—dc23
  [B]
                          2014044982

Printed in the United States of America

This book is dedicated to my mother, who, when times were difficult, bought me my first books. Additionally, a special thank you to my wife Pamela along with teachers Caria Kennedy and Pam Hammen, who assisted in the production of this work.

Contents

Preface

Hello there,

The president of the United States is the most powerful office in the world. It comes with a great deal of responsibility and decision making about many different matters.

Each of our presidents has been unique. They also had special talents that may not have been written about in your other books.

There is a story about each of them where you might be able to learn a lesson that could help you in the future. Some will make you laugh, but read or listen carefully, because you might discover that you and some of the presidents have some things in common.

The answer key can be found at the end of the book.

President George Washington during the American Revolution

CHAPTER 1

George Washington
The 1st President
1789–1797
Jack Goes to the Circus

Being the president of the United States is a job that keeps a person very busy. However, even as the leader of the country, George Washington would find some time to relax. One of his favorite ways to do this was to attend the circus. As an expert rider, he especially enjoyed acts that featured horses.

This was the first circus in the United States, and it was created by John Bill Ricketts. The show was located in the city of Philadelphia, which served as the nation's capital while Mr. Washington was president. The first circus performance in America took place on April 3, 1793.

The two men became friends and would sometimes go riding together in the countryside. Shortly before the president retired, he sold one of his favorite horses, Jack, to Mr. Ricketts for $150. Jack was twenty-eight years old, and President Washington had ridden him when he was a general during the American Revolution. Because so many people wanted to see Jack, he became a star of the circus for the next several years.

TODAY'S QUESTIONS

1. In what city did the first circus take place?
2. How much money did President Washington receive when he sold Jack to Mr. Ricketts?
3. What was the name of the war in which President Washington rode Jack?

1

President John Adams by Alonzo Chappel (1735–1826)

Chapter 2

John Adams
The 2nd President
1797–1801
Lost in the Woods

Have you ever gotten lost? It's nothing to be ashamed of, because almost everybody has been at one time or another. But what happens when a member of the First Family gets lost?

It would be difficult for that to happen today because they are guarded by the Secret Service. But it did take place many years ago.

On November 1, 1800, John Adams became the first president to move into the White House, although the builders hadn't finished it. Some of the mansion's construction had not been completed, and the paint was still wet on the walls in some of the rooms.

Two weeks later, President Adams's wife Abigail arrived from their home in Massachusetts. However, her carriage was lost in the woods for two hours until the driver was able to find his way back to the main road. In those days, there were no Secret Service agents to protect the First Family.

Mrs. Adams called the White House "the great castle," but she and her husband didn't enjoy living there, as they found it to be a cold and damp place. She even used one large area that was unfinished, now known as the East Room, to dry their clothes.

The couple only lived there for five months until Thomas Jefferson became the new president. At that point they returned to their farm in Massachusetts, where they spent the rest of their lives.

1. Who was the first president to move into the White House?
2. What did Mrs. Adams call the White House?
3. What group protects the First Family?

CHAPTER 3

Thomas Jefferson
The 3rd President
1801–1809
Jurassic Jefferson

Of all of the presidents, Thomas Jefferson was one of the smartest and most creative. He wrote most of the Declaration of Independence, spoke six languages, played the violin, and had his own library, which had more than ten thousand books.

President Jefferson also had a rather unusual hobby. Even though he wasn't a scientist, he enjoyed studying dinosaur fossils. This is known as paleontology.

Before becoming president, he learned about a place in Kentucky called Big Bone Lick that was known to have fossils of dinosaurs and other beasts. Many of them had died there more than ten thousand years ago during the Ice Age.

In 1803, President Jefferson sent the famous explorer Meriwether Lewis to Big Bone Lick to bring back some of the fossils. He collected many bones and had them shipped to the White House on a riverboat. But President Jefferson never got them because the boat sank in the Missis-sippi River. However, he didn't give up.

Four years later, in 1807, the president sent Mr. Lewis's partner, Wil-liam Clark, to Big Bone Lick to gather more samples. He found so many old bones in just three weeks that he was able to ship three huge boxes to Washington, D.C. In fact, there were enough fossils that President Jeffer-son laid them out in a special room in the White House in order to display his new collection.

In 1849, after President Jefferson had passed away, some of the fossils were given to the Academy of Natural Sciences in Philadelphia, where more than fifty bones from the collection remain today.

President Thomas Jefferson

TODAY'S QUESTIONS

1. Where did President Jefferson send Lewis and Clark to collect dinosaur bones?
2. What happened to the first shipment of fossils?
3. What is another term for an old bone?

President James Madison

Chapter 4

James Madison
The 4th President
1809–1817
What Is for Dessert?

Do you like ice cream? If so, what is your favorite flavor?

The fourth president of the United States, James Madison, and First Lady Dolley enjoyed ice cream so much that they had it served to their guests following dinners at the White House. One of the most popular desserts that they offered was called strawberry "bombe glacée."

It was made from frozen cream, sugar, and fruit and had been created by a former slave named Sallie Shadd. When Mrs. Madison traveled to Delaware to taste Sallie's ice cream creation, she liked it so much that it soon became the official White House dessert.

But that wasn't Mrs. Madison's favorite ice cream dish. The one that she enjoyed most was made with oysters that were caught in the Potomac River near the White House. An oyster is a type of seafood with a hard shell.

Also, there were no freezers in those days, so ice cream had to be kept in an icehouse with large blocks of ice cut from frozen water, where it was packed on straw and held in a cool place.

TODAY'S QUESTIONS

1. Who was Dolley Madison?
2. Who was Sallie Shadd?
3. What was Mrs. Madison's favorite flavor of ice cream?

President James Monroe

Chapter 5

James Monroe
The 5th President
1817–1825
The Night the Argument Was Settled

Sometimes when there is an argument between two people, a third person has to step in to help settle it. That is what happened one evening to President James Monroe at a White House dinner.

It all began when the staff put together the seating chart for a banquet. They placed the representatives of England and France across from each other at the same table. This was a big mistake, because these two countries had been enemies for many, many years.

At the dinner, the British official noticed that the French representative would bite at his thumb whenever he made a remark. He considered this act to be an insult and finally asked, "Do you bite your thumb at me, sir?"

"I do," replied the hotshot Frenchman.

The two angry men left the dining area and went into another room followed by President Monroe. The two officials drew their swords and prepared to fight a duel, which was legal in many parts of America in the early 1800s. But before they could attack each other, the president drew his own sword and stepped between the men, stopping the duel.

President Monroe knew a thing or two about fighting. He had served in George Washington's army during the American Revolution and was severely wounded at the Battle of Trenton (New Jersey). On that evening, the American leader was in no mood for the men to settle their differences with weapons inside the White House.

After preventing the fight, President Madison called for their carriages and sent each of them back to his home. That's why it sometimes takes a third person to settle an argument.

Someday you might be the one who has to settle an argument between two friends. Don't use a sword; the power of your good words should be enough to get the job done.

TODAY'S QUESTIONS

1. From what countries were the two officials who were going to fight the duel?
2. In whose army did President Monroe serve during the American Revolution?
3. Where did the banquet take place?

CHAPTER 6

John Quincy Adams
The 6th President
1825–1829
The Leaking Boat

You may have been told that whenever you go swimming or go out on a boat, you should always take along a friend. That is good advice, and one president found it out the hard way.

On June 13, 1825, President John Quincy Adams and his friend Antoine Giusta, a member of the White House staff, decided to go canoeing on Tiber Creek in Washington, D.C. Mr. Adams was the first son of a former president (John Adams) to be elected to the same position and had only been in office for a few weeks.

As the new president and Antoine began to row across the creek, they realized that their small boat was in bad condition and was beginning to leak. There were additional problems for the two men, as the winds were beginning to blow more strongly.

There were no life jackets onboard so, as the canoe was sinking, they decided to jump overboard and swim to the shore. The president's son John had been waiting for them on the other side and helped the men to safety.

A short while later, a carriage arrived to take them back to their families at the White House.

So the next time you're planning to have fun on the water, remember the story about President John Quincy Adams and his friend Antoine. Always play it safe, and if you're on a boat, remember your life jacket.

President John Quincy Adams

TODAY'S QUESTIONS

1. Who was President Adams's friend who went canoeing with him?
2. What happened to the canoe?
3. How did the president and Antoine get to the shore?

President Andrew Jackson

CHAPTER 7

Andrew Jackson

The 7th President

1829–1837

More Cheese, Please!

When you are the president of the United States, you receive some strange gifts from the citizens. One of the most bizarre went to Andrew Jackson.

In 1835, he received a huge, 1,400-pound cheese wheel from New York dairy farmer Colonel Thomas S. Meacham. It was four feet around and two feet thick, sealed in a giant wrapper with the patriotic slogan, "The Union, it must be Preserved."

In 1837, with just two weeks left in his last term as president, Mr. Jackson decided that the large piece of cheese had to go, and he had an idea how to do it. On February 22, he held a public gathering at the White House, where visitors were greeted by the massive cheese wheel that was sitting in the main entryway into the mansion. Those attending were told to eat as much cheese as they wished, and they did. About ten thousand people attended the event, and after two hours, the cheese was gone.

However, two weeks later when the new president, Martin Van Buren, and his family moved into the White House, it took several days for the staff to get the smell of cheese out of the mansion and its furniture.

Also, Andrew Jackson wasn't the first president to receive a cheese wheel as a gift. In 1802, Thomas Jefferson got one that weighed 1,235 pounds from the citizens of Cheshire, Massachusetts. Too bad someone didn't donate some macaroni!

Let the party begin as citizens dig into the giant cheese wheel. (Benjamin Perley Poore, 1886)

TODAY'S QUESTIONS

1. What did President Jackson do to get rid of the giant cheese wheel?
2. How long did it take the citizens to eat all of the cheese?
3. Who was the other president who had received a cheese wheel as a gift?

CHAPTER 8

Martin Van Buren
The 8th President
1837–1841
I'm O.K.

Have you ever said "O.K." to answer a question? As an example, someone may have asked you how your day at school was, and you said, "O.K."

Did you ever wonder where the term *O.K.* came from? It actually has something to do with our eighth president, Martin Van Buren.

In 1840, he was running for reelection. During the campaign, many citizens called him by his nickname, "Old Kinderhook," after his birthplace in New York State. His supporters formed the "O.K. Club" and could be heard shouting "Vote for O.K." in a shorter form of his nickname.

Over time, *O.K.* came to mean "all right." But things didn't go O.K. for Martin Van Buren in 1840, as he lost the election and a chance for a second term as president.

TODAY'S QUESTIONS

1. What was President Van Buren's nickname?
2. What does O.K. mean today?
3. How did President Van Buren do in the election of 1840?

President Martin Van Buren

CHAPTER 9

William Henry Harrison
The 9th President
1841
Almost a Doctor

Of all the jobs out there, most of our presidents were lawyers before they were elected. In fact, of the forty-four presidents, twenty-six have been lawyers. Some, like Abraham Lincoln and Franklin Roosevelt, are among the most famous.

But only one president studied to become a doctor. Do you know who he was?

It was our ninth president, William Henry Harrison. In 1790, seventeen-year-old William entered the University of Pennsylvania to begin his studies as a doctor. The university was started by Benjamin Franklin and was the first to have a college that trained doctors.

William studied medicine under Dr. Benjamin Rush, one of America's Founding Fathers. But after his own father died in 1791, there was no money left for him to continue his education, so he was forced to leave the college.

At that point, he chose a different path and joined the military, where he became a hero in the War of 1812. He was presented the Congressional Gold Medal for his service.

But not everyone believed in William Henry Harrison as a soldier. In 1795, he met and fell in love with Anna Symmes and wanted to marry her. But her father was an important judge who refused to give William permission to wed his daughter because soldiers didn't make much money. So they waited until the judge left town on a business trip, and they ran away and got married.

President William Henry Harrison

It worked out pretty well, because they were married for forty-six years and had ten children! Their grandson Benjamin grew up and became president in 1889.

For William Henry Harrison, his life may have gone a different way than his plan to be a doctor, but through hard work and goodwill, everything came out for the best, and in 1840, he was elected president of the United States.

TODAY'S QUESTIONS

1. What was William Henry Harrison studying to be in college?
2. What did he do when he left college?
3. Why didn't Anna's father want her to marry William?

President John Tyler

CHAPTER 10

John Tyler
The 10th President
1841–1845
It Was a Very Unusual Year

The term of a president is four years unless something happens to that person. For some, their final year in office wasn't very exciting because there wasn't much going on. But that wasn't so for John Tyler.

President Tyler's final full year in office was exciting and quite busy. It started on February 28, 1844, when he and a number of other officials were aboard the battleship *USS Princeton*. The weather was good on that day as they cruised the Potomac River in Washington, D.C.

The captain wanted to fire the ship's new cannons even though they had not been tested. That was a big mistake, as one of the cannons exploded. However, President Tyler had luck on his side that day and was not hurt.

Shortly after the accident, the president decided to marry his girlfriend Julia Gardiner, but they didn't want a big wedding. That's pretty tough to do, because whatever the president does gets a lot of attention.

On June 26, 1844, President Tyler and his bodyguards snuck out of the White House and went to New York City. It was there that he and Julia had a private wedding with just friends and family. They were able to keep it secret so that newspaper reporters didn't know that they were getting married.

From being on a ship where a cannon exploded to having a secret wedding, you could say that in President Tyler's last year in office, you could always expect the unexpected to take place.

Today's Questions

1. How many years is one term as president? Is it two, three, or four years?
2. What happened aboard the ship that President Tyler was visiting?
3. Why did President Tyler and Julia keep their wedding a secret?

CHAPTER 11

James K. Polk
The 11th President
1845–1849
Always Keep Your Word

It's always important to keep your promises. Why? Because it means that other people can trust you when you tell them something.

When a person runs for president, they usually make many promises to the voters, although sometimes it's tough to keep those promises. It's not because the president is a bad person, but quite often other things might happen that keep him from being able to do what he promised. One example is if the United States uses money to build a bridge, we might not have enough left to build a road even if the president promised to build it.

However, in 1844 when James K. Polk was running for president, he made the voters a promise that no candidate had made before. He told them that if they elected him, he would only serve one term and not run for reelection. Not even George Washington had ever made such an offer.

That was a big promise, because most presidents run for a second term. One of them was Franklin Roosevelt, who was elected to four terms in office.

The voters took Mr. Polk at his word, and in 1844, he was elected president of the United States. Over the next four years, things went well, and many people asked him to run again.

But he had made a promise, and he stuck to it. After his term was over, President Polk and his wife left Washington, D.C., and moved to their new home in Nashville, Tennessee.

Sometimes things might happen where you are not able to keep a promise, but if you can, be like President James K. Polk and keep your word. In the end, it will always earn you the respect of others.

President James K. Polk

TODAY'S QUESTIONS

1. What did President Polk promise the voters in 1844?
2. Did he keep his promise?
3. Why is keeping a promise important?

President Zachary Taylor

CHAPTER 12

Zachary Taylor

The 12th President

1848–1850

Always a Soldier

Voting is one of the rights that Americans enjoy under our set of laws known as the Constitution. A person is not forced to vote in our country, and you will be able to make that choice when you become eighteen years old. Until then, you will get to vote in elections that take place at your school.

During an election, the people running for office spend a great deal of time campaigning. A campaign is made up of a series of events where a candidate for president appears before the voters at different places, hoping to convince them to vote for him or her.

Today, the campaigns for those who are running for president cost a great deal of money. They have to pay for things like travel, meals, radio and television ads, and the salaries of their staff. In 2012, President Obama's campaign spent $1 billion to get him reelected.

But imagine if a person could get elected president by doing only a little bit of campaigning and spending a small amount of money! Is it possible? It's true, it actually did happen.

In 1848, Zachary Taylor was elected president of the United States without much of a campaign. He had never held an office before, because for forty years, he had been in the U.S. Army. During President Taylor's military career, he fought in four wars, which made him very popular with most of the American people.

General Taylor had been selected to run for president but did not know for more than a month if he was an official candidate. The reason was that the letter that gave him the good news had been sitting in a post office for six weeks, because the person who mailed it forgot to put a stamp on it! Remember that in 1848, there was no e-mail, Twitter, or cell phones. If you needed to get some information to a person, you had to mail them a letter.

In fact, President Taylor had never voted before 1848, as he had not lived in one place long enough to be eligible to do so. When he did vote for the first time, he was sixty-four years old and like other candidates, he voted for himself.

As he moved to Washington, D.C., the new president brought along his favorite horse "Old Whitey," whom he had ridden in many battles over the years. The old horse would spend his days eating the grass from the White House lawn as people would walk by to get a look at him.

Voting is one of our rights, and as President Taylor proved, you're never too old to start voting.

TODAY'S QUESTIONS

1. What was Zachary Taylor's job before he was president?
2. What is a campaign?
3. Who was "Old Whitey"?

CHAPTER 13

Millard Fillmore

The 13th President

1850–1853

Where Are the Books?

Millard Fillmore became president in 1850, but when he and his family moved into the White House, they noticed something was missing. The most famous mansion in America had no books!

Eleven other presidents had lived in the White House, but none had placed any books in the library that was upstairs. When the new president and his wife Abigail saw that there were no books on the shelves, they quickly set about to change that.

President Fillmore asked Congress for $2,250 to buy books for the White House library. When the money was approved, the first three books that were ordered were a dictionary, an atlas, and the Bible. In all, the Fillmores bought about two hundred books for the library. The president would always try to spend an hour reading in the room after his workday was finished. Today, the White House library has almost 2,500 books.

The following year, the president helped save many books. On Christmas Eve 1851, a spark from one of the chimneys at the Library of Congress building, where a large number of volumes were stored, started a fire in the building. When they were told about the blaze, President Fillmore and members of his cabinet rushed three miles to get there and started a bucket brigade to help the fire department. A bucket brigade was a line of people who would pass pails of water from one to another to help put out a fire.

Two-thirds of the Library of Congress's fifty-five thousand books, including many that had been bought from Thomas Jefferson, were destroyed by the fire. But part of the collection was saved because of

President Millard Fillmore

the quick action of President Fillmore and others. The Library of Congress was rebuilt after the fire, and today thousands of people visit there each year.

Today's Questions

1. How many books were in the library when the Fillmores moved into the White House?
2. What happened at the Library of Congress on Christmas Eve 1851?
3. What is a bucket brigade?

President Franklin Pierce

CHAPTER 14

Franklin Pierce
The 14th President
1853–1857
Please Pay Attention

Whenever you are doing something, it's always important to pay attention. It's just safer that way.

Before the car was invented, most people rode horses as their main way to travel. That included the presidents.

Most believe that George Washington was the best horseman of all of the presidents. There were several others who were very good, and among those was the 14th president, Franklin Pierce. He had been in the Army and was a top rider, but even so, he once had an accident.

Shortly after moving into the White House in 1853, he was riding back to the mansion one evening after visiting a friend. Suddenly, his horse struck an older woman named Mrs. Lewis, who had stepped into the street. President Pierce was arrested by the police because of his reckless riding, but the charges were soon dropped.

Mrs. Lewis was not hurt in the accident, but this story proves why it's always important to pay attention to what you are doing.

TODAY'S QUESTIONS

1. Which president was considered to have been the best horse rider?
2. Who was the president who had a horse-riding accident?
3. What happened to Mrs. Lewis after she was struck by the horse?

President James Buchanan

CHAPTER 15

James Buchanan

The 15th President

1857–1861

Freedom for All

James Buchanan was president from 1857 to 1861. This was a very difficult time, because much of the nation was divided over the issue of slavery. Even though many citizens wanted it to continue, President Buchanan knew that to hold another person as a slave was wrong, and he wanted to do something about it.

As a young man, he came up with an idea in 1832 when his sister Harriet married Robert Henry of Virginia, which at the time was a slave state. Mr. Buchanan discovered that his new brother-in-law's family owned slaves, so he purchased two of the females. Afterward, he took them to his home state of Pennsylvania, which didn't have slavery, where they were released and given their freedom.

It was learned that over the years, he bought several more slaves with his own money while he was president and also sent them to Pennsylvania, where they were set free. Since he didn't brag about his good deeds, many people were unaware of President Buchanan's kindness until a number of years later.

Always remember, if you do a good deed, you don't have to brag about it, because a good deed always speaks for itself.

TODAY'S QUESTIONS

1. Who was the president who bought slaves and then set them free?
2. Was Virginia a free state or a slave state?
3. Where did President Buchanan send the slaves to be free?

President Abraham Lincoln

CHAPTER 16

Abraham Lincoln
The 16th President
1861–1865
The Champion

Wrestling is the world's oldest sport. It dates back thousands of years to the days of the ancient Greeks and Romans. Since then, the United States has produced many great wrestlers, such as Olympic champions Dan Gable and John Smith.

But did you know about the president who was a great wrestler?

In the 1800s, there were no high school or college wrestling teams, so the top wrestlers would travel from town to town taking on challengers. There was a young man who lived in New Salem, Illinois, who at one time was the champion of his county. He stood six feet, four inches and weighed 180 pounds. Although he was slender, he was very strong and skillful.

In twelve years, the young man lost just one match. He was so good that many years later, he was chosen to be in the National Wrestling Hall of Fame in Oklahoma.

But the man from Illinois wasn't just a good athlete, he was also very bright. He studied hard and became a lawyer. In 1860, the former wrestler was elected president of the United States.

Who was he? He is the man who is seen today on the $5 bill . . . Abraham Lincoln!

TODAY'S QUESTIONS

1. What is the world's oldest sport?
2. In what state did Lincoln live while he was wrestling?
3. What was Lincoln's job before he became president?

President Andrew Johnson

CHAPTER 17

Andrew Johnson
The 17th President
1865–1869
It's Never Too Late to Learn

Getting a good education is important. A major part of that is learning to read. Your teacher is currently helping you to become a better reader with classroom activities.

However, there was once a young man from North Carolina who didn't have a chance to go to school. His name was Andrew Johnson.

Andrew's parents were poor, and when he was ten years old, they sent him to work at a tailor shop to learn how to make clothes. But he still wanted to learn how to read and write.

Over time, he learned how to read with the help of one of the shop's customers, Dr. William Hill, who would often read to the workers as they sewed clothes. Andrew enjoyed the book *The American Speaker* so much that Dr. Hill gave it to him as a gift.

In 1827, Andrew married Eliza McCardle, who was well educated and helped him improve his reading along with his math and writing skills. Did his education help him in life? He went on to become the governor of Tennessee, a congressman, a senator, the vice president, and the president.

When he died in 1875, he was buried with a copy of the U.S. Constitution, which he had learned to read. President Johnson showed the public that it's never too late to learn.

TODAY'S QUESTIONS

1. Andrew Johnson was from what state?
2. What does a tailor do?
3. What was buried with President Johnson?

President Ulysses S. Grant

CHAPTER 18

Ulysses S. Grant
The 18th President
1869–1877
Honesty Is the Best Policy

Ulysses S. Grant was an American hero. In 1865, he was the winning general of the Civil War, which freed the slaves. Three years later, he was elected president of the United States. But even though he had achieved great things in his life, he didn't believe that made him better than everyone else.

Not everything that President Grant did was good. In fact, he had one bad habit that would often get him in trouble. He enjoyed driving fast.

This was before the invention of the car, but the president enjoyed doing his speeding through Washington, D.C., in his horse-drawn carriage.

One day while swiftly moving over the streets of the nation's capital, President Grant was pulled over by police officer William West, who was on his horse. He asked, "Well, officer, what do you want with me?"

"Mr. President," answered the policeman, "I want to tell you that you were violating the law by driving at a reckless speed. Your fast driving, sir, has set the example for a lot of other gentlemen."

The president apologized and, like most of today's drivers, promised to slow down. However, the very next day, the war hero was once again in his carriage speeding through the busy streets. Officer West recognized the famous coach and, as he had done the day before, signaled the driver to pull over and stop.

As the policeman again approached, Grant politely asked, "Do you think, officer, that I was violating the speed laws?"

"I certainly do, Mr. President," answered the policeman. "I cautioned you yesterday, Mr. President, about fast driving, and you said, sir, that it would not occur again. I am very sorry, Mr. President, to have to do it, for you are the nation's chief executive, but my duty is plain, sir: I shall have to place you under arrest!"

The president knew that he was wrong and didn't argue with the policeman.

At that point, Officer West drove the carriage along with the president to the station house. He was charged with speeding and paid a $5 fine. The police department held on to the carriage, and President Grant walked back to the White House. As time passed, he and Officer West became good friends.

A few years later, following his presidency, Grant broke another law but once again proved his honesty. He was on vacation in McKean County, Pennsylvania, when he became aware that he had been fishing out of season. At that point, he went to the office of the justice of the peace and insisted on paying the fine, which he did even though no one had seen him break the law.

President Grant's actions proved what Benjamin Franklin once said: "Honesty is the best policy."

TODAY'S QUESTIONS

1. Why did President Grant have to pay a $5 fine?
2. What law did President Grant break while he was on vacation in Pennsylvania?
3. Who said that "honesty is the best policy"?

CHAPTER 19

Rutherford B. Hayes
The 19th President
1877–1881
Tradition

What is a tradition? That's when you begin doing something and it continues to take place for many years.

Part of the tradition of Easter is the Easter Bunny. He started out in 1682 in Germany and has been around every year since then.

In Washington, D.C., there's another tradition that's also been around for a long time. It's called the White House Easter Egg Roll, and it has always been held the day after Easter.

It began after the Civil War in the 1860s. Local children would roll Easter eggs on the grounds of the Capitol Building. But by 1876, congressmen were growing upset at the crowds and the mess that they left behind, so they passed a law where kids couldn't use the Capitol grounds as a play area.

In 1877, Rutherford B. Hayes took office as the nation's 19th president. He had been a hero in the Civil War and loved kids. He and his wife had eight children of their own, but most were already adults when he was elected president.

On Easter day in 1878, President Hayes was riding in his carriage past the Capitol Building when he saw some children who had been crying. That was because they couldn't roll their Easter eggs since the new law had been passed by Congress. The president stopped his carriage and spoke with them for a few minutes. He then invited the group to play with their eggs on the White House lawn, which they did.

That was the start of a new tradition, the White House Easter Egg Roll. It has continued to grow since it began under President and Mrs. Hayes in 1878.

President Rutherford B. Hayes

Children attending the annual White House Easter Egg Roll

Today nearly thirty thousand people take part in the event each year with one important rule: at least one child from each of the fifty states must take part.

This is a fun and proud tradition that President Hayes saved when he invited the children to bring their Easter eggs to the White House lawn.

TODAY'S QUESTIONS

1. What is a tradition?
2. Why did the children have to stop playing with their eggs near the Capitol Building?
3. What did President Hayes tell the children when he stopped his carriage?

President James Garfield

CHAPTER 20

James Garfield
The 20th President
1881
The Incredible Mr. Garfield

Whenever a person is running for president, it gives the voters a chance to get to know that man or woman. However, during the election of 1880, the citizens were getting to know one of the most unique candidates to ever run for the office.

His name was James Garfield, and he had been a general during the Civil War. But he was also a man of peace, having been a minister. The former soldier is the only president ever to have been a preacher.

Mr. Garfield was also ambidextrous, which means that he could write with either hand. But he didn't just write with both hands. Mr. Garfield could write in Latin with one hand and in Greek with the other, at the same time! When he would do that while visiting with the voters, they were amazed and entertained.

He was also the first president to give speeches during a campaign in two languages—English and German. This was very helpful, as a number of citizens from Germany had arrived in the United States but still spoke their home language.

There was no doubt that James Garfield was a smart man, but he also stayed in shape. To build his muscles, he juggled Indian clubs (shaped like bowling pins) as part of his exercise program.

All of those talents paid off, as James Garfield won the election of 1880.

TODAY'S QUESTIONS

1. What does the term *ambidextrous* mean?
2. What were the two languages, other than English, that President Garfield could write?
3. What was the language, other than English, that President Garfield spoke during his campaign?

CHAPTER 21

Chester Arthur

The 21st President

1881–1885

A Sharp-Dressed Man

Have you ever been told to put on clean clothes? Has anyone ever taught you how to wash your clothes?

Most of our presidents have dressed well. As citizens, that's what we expect from them. It would look funny if the president went into an important meeting wearing a T-shirt and flip-flops. Most people will give you more respect when you are able to dress nicely.

So who was our best-dressed president? Many believe that it was Chester Arthur. He was a stylish dresser and enjoyed the latest fashions.

President Arthur spent quite a bit of money for clothes, because he didn't buy his in a regular store like most people. He had them custom made by his own tailor in New York City. When they were ready, the tailor would send them to the White House. The president had eighty suits in his closets.

He had two nicknames—"The Gentleman Boss" and "Elegant Arthur." It was not unusual for the president to change his outfits several times a day. He had a special person at the White House whose only job was to help prepare his clothes.

President Arthur was also one of those people who kept late hours. He would often, along with his Secret Service agents, take walks in Washington, D.C., after midnight. Today presidents are not allowed to do that because it is too dangerous.

So the next time you're told to put on clean clothes—remember President Chester Arthur.

President Chester Arthur

TODAY'S QUESTIONS

1. Where was the tailor located who made President Arthur's clothes?
2. How many suits did President Arthur own?
3. What is it that President Arthur enjoyed doing after midnight?

President Grover Cleveland

CHAPTER 22

Grover Cleveland
The 22nd and 24th President
1885–1889 (1st term), 1893–1897 (2nd term)
Believe in Yourself

Grover Cleveland did something that no other president has ever done. He became president, then he lost his reelection. He then ran again four years later and won again. Here's how he did it.

In 1884, Mr. Cleveland, who had been the governor of New York, ran for president. He easily won the election, becoming the nation's 22nd president.

In 1888, President Cleveland ran for reelection against Benjamin Harrison but lost. However, that didn't discourage him or the First Lady. As they were packing up their belongings in the White House, Frances Cleveland told the staff, "Take care of the place, we'll be back."

There's no doubt that she believed in her husband and his ability to come back to get reelected. And she was right.

In 1892, former president Cleveland defeated President Harrison to win the election. He became the first person in history to win, then lose, and then rewin the presidency.

And it proved that Frances Cleveland was right when she told her staff four years earlier, "We'll be back!"

The victory by the Clevelands in 1892 is a good lesson to always believe in yourself. When he left office for good in 1897, President Cleveland said, "I have always tried to do what is right."

Today's Questions

1. Before he became president the first time, Grover Cleveland had been the governor of what state?
2. What did Mrs. Cleveland tell the White House staff after her husband lost the election?
3. What did President Cleveland say that he always tried to do?

Chapter 23

Benjamin Harrison
The 23rd President
1889–1893
Someone, Turn Out the Lights!

In 1888, there were many people who weren't surprised when Benjamin Harrison was elected president of the United States. Why? That is because several members of his family were already famous leaders.

His father John had been a congressman, and his grandfather was William Henry Harrison, the 9th president of the United States. Benjamin was seven years old when his grandfather was elected president, and before that, his great-grandfather signed the Declaration of Independence. The Harrisons are one of the most well-known families in American history.

Have you ever been told to turn out the lights?

Just before President Harrison and his family moved into the White House, electric lighting was installed. The new system replaced the old gaslights that had been there for years. Wires were buried in the walls with round switches placed in each room for turning the current on and off.

But the president and Mrs. Harrison didn't trust the new system and refused to use the switches because of their fear of being shocked. They would either have the staff operate the switches or, on some nights, they would just leave the lights on.

However, today we always turn out the lights to save money on electricity.

Also, there were many presidents who wore a beard, but Benjamin Harrison was the last to wear one while serving in the office.

President Benjamin Harrison

TODAY'S QUESTIONS

1. Who was Benjamin Harrison's grandfather?
2. What type of power was used to run the White House's new lighting system?
3. Why didn't the Harrisons turn out the lights in the White House?

President William McKinley

CHAPTER 24

William McKinley
The 25th President
1897–1901
Always Win with Kindness

Have you ever gotten angry with someone? If so, what did you do about it?

William McKinley was known as a very kind man. Years before he was president, he was running for Congress in his home state of Ohio.

There was a newspaper reporter who would follow him to every town where he would go. He would then write a story trying to make Mr. McKinley look bad in the eyes of the voters.

However, the reporter became ill as the campaign continued, and he was getting worse and worse. One night Mr. McKinley was inside a carriage going to a nearby town to give a speech. The weather was very bad—cold and windy.

As the horses trotted along, Mr. McKinley heard something outside the carriage that sounded like someone coughing. He asked the driver to stop and got out into the cold night's air. Mr. McKinley looked at the man riding next to the driver, and it was the newspaper reporter.

"Get down off that seat, young man," he said as he removed his coat. "You put on this overcoat and get into the carriage."

The reporter did as he was told, using Mr. McKinley's coat to get warm as he made his way into the carriage.

Once inside, the reporter said, "I guess you don't know who I am. I have been with you the whole campaign, giving it to you every time you spoke, and I am going over tonight to rip you to pieces if I can."

"I know," said Mr. McKinley kindly. "But you get inside and get warm, so that you can do a good job."

Sometimes people will do or say mean things because they've never been treated with kindness. On that night, future president William

McKinley knew that even though the reporter had written some harsh words about him, the only way to help the reporter to change his ways was to offer a kind hand.

A writer named Henry James once said, "Three things in human life are important: the first is to be kind; the second is to be kind; and the third is to be kind."

TODAY'S QUESTIONS

1. Was Mr. McKinley riding in a carriage or on a train?
2. What did Mr. McKinley give to the newspaper reporter?
3. Did the story take place in Oregon or Ohio?

CHAPTER 25

Theodore Roosevelt
The 26th President
1901–1909
Saving the Land

Have you seen some trash on the ground and picked it up, then thrown it away? Most of us have done that at one time or another because we want to keep our areas looking clean and nice.

Before there were programs to protect the planet, there was Theodore Roosevelt. In his days before becoming president, Mr. Roosevelt traveled to many parts of the western United States. It bothered him that a great deal of land was being destroyed because it wasn't being cared for. Also, there were shortages of some animals, like the bison, because there were no limits on hunting back then.

Mr. Roosevelt enjoyed hunting, but he knew that there had to be limits so that the animals wouldn't become extinct. He also knew that ranchers needed to do a better job with their cattle herds so that the grasslands would be able to grow.

In 1901, when he became president, Mr. Roosevelt wasted little time using his power to protect the wildlife and public lands. He created the U.S. Forest Service and . . .

- 51 federal bird reservations
- 4 national game preserves
- 150 national forests
- 5 national parks
- 18 national monuments, including the Grand Canyon.

President Theodore Roosevelt at Yosemite National Park

During his presidency, Theodore Roosevelt protected approximately 230 million acres of public land. Today we can visit all of these places because of his work.

TODAY'S QUESTIONS

1. Why did President Roosevelt want limits on hunting?
2. Did President Roosevelt make the Grand Canyon a national monument?
3. Are we allowed to visit the public lands that were protected by President Roosevelt?

President William Howard Taft

CHAPTER 26

William Howard Taft
The 27th President
1909–1913
It Is Better to Give than to Receive

Christmas is a time of giving. There is little doubt that no other president enjoyed that purpose more than William Howard Taft.

The first reason is because many citizens thought that President Taft looked a lot like Santa Claus. He was six feet tall and weighed 350 pounds. The only thing that was missing was a white beard and a red suit.

Presidents are always receiving gifts from people around the world. Remember those giant cheese wheels that were given to Thomas Jefferson and Andrew Jackson? But President Taft enjoyed giving gifts rather than receiving them.

Each year, it would take him several days to complete his Christmas shopping. His favorite gifts that he gave were books and jewelry. He would also include a handwritten note with every Christmas card that he mailed. Can you imagine receiving a handwritten Christmas card from the president of the United States?

Also, President Taft always took care of his staff at the White House during the holidays. He would give a Christmas turkey to all married White House workers—that was usually just over one hundred turkeys that would cost him a total of about $400. He would also give special gifts to the Secret Service agents who worked to protect him.

In 1909, the Taft family displayed the first Christmas tree in the Blue Room of the White House. That tradition still takes place today.

On his final evening as president in 1913, Mr. Taft stayed awake most of the night signing his name to hundreds of pieces of paper for people who had asked for his autograph. He then placed them in envelopes that were mailed the next day. Even on his last night as president, he felt that it was better to give than to receive.

Today's Questions

1. What did President Taft do with every Christmas card before it was mailed?
2. What did President Taft give as gifts to the White House staff?
3. What did President Taft do on his last night in the White House?

CHAPTER 27

Woodrow Wilson
The 28th President
1913–1921
Never Give Up

Do you know someone who has trouble reading? It doesn't mean that they are stupid. In fact, they may be quite bright, but they could have what is known as a learning difficulty.

Everybody's brain works differently. Some people learn quickly, while it takes longer for others. Once upon a time, there was a president who had a learning difficulty.

His name was Woodrow Wilson, and he struggled to learn his letters. Because of his learning difficulty, he would see the letters on a page differently than most students. Some were turned around or upside down.

Woodrow worked hard and, over time, his reading got better. When he was twelve years old, he could read most books, but he had to do it slowly so that he could understand all of the words. He also worked hard on his speaking skills, which helped him in school.

Did it work? He graduated from high school and college and then became a college professor. He also wrote a book about George Washington. Years later, Mr. Wilson was elected governor of New Jersey, and in 1912, he was voted president of the United States.

While he was president, he helped lead America to victory in World War I.

President Wilson once said, "The difference between a strong man and a weak one is that the strong one does not give up after a defeat."

For a person who couldn't read until he was twelve years old, Woodrow Wilson did pretty well because he never gave up.

President Woodrow Wilson

Today's Questions

1. Why couldn't Woodrow Wilson learn to read when he was a child?
2. Woodrow Wilson once wrote a book. Who was it about?
3. Did Woodrow Wilson give up when he had trouble reading?

President Warren Harding with his dog Laddie Boy

CHAPTER 28

Warren Harding
The 29th President
1921–1923
The President's Best Friend

Do you have a dog? If so, what breed is he or she? What is his or her name?

Many of our presidents' dogs have become celebrities in their own right. In 1990, First Lady Barbara Bush wrote a book about the family's springer spaniel, Millie.

When the Harding family arrived at the White House in 1921, they brought their Airedale terrier with them from their home in Ohio. In a short time, he became nearly as well known as the president. His name was Laddie Boy.

The years of the 1920s were a good time to be a dog. The most popular was a German shepherd named Rin Tin Tin. He became a movie star and was in twenty-seven films. At one point, Rin Tin Tin was earning $6,000 per week!

Laddie Boy wasn't making money like Rin Tin Tin, but he did get to live in the White House and have special meals prepared for him. The kitchen staff would give a birthday party each year he was there.

Wherever one would find President Harding, Laddie Boy was usually close by. Whether the president was playing golf, working in his office, or holding an important meeting, the loyal dog was near his master's side. Laddie even had his own seat in the room where the country's most important leaders would meet with the president.

When President Harding died in 1923, his wife gave Laddie Boy to the Secret Service agent who had been assigned to protect her. The former presidential pet lived out the rest of his days with the agent's family at their home in Massachusetts.

To honor President Harding, more than nineteen thousand newsboys throughout the nation each donated a penny to create a statue of Laddie Boy. The pennies were melted down and molded into a life-size likeness of the famous pooch. Today the statue is one of the many items at the National Museum of American History in Washington, D.C.

TODAY'S QUESTIONS

1. What was the name of President Harding's dog?
2. What was the name of the dog that was a big movie star in the 1920s?
3. What was used to make the statue of Laddie Boy?

CHAPTER 29

Calvin Coolidge
The 30th President
1923–1929
The President and the Burglar

Have you ever made a mistake and someone forgave you for it? One of the kindest things that a person can do is to forgive a person when they've done something wrong.

In 1923, shortly after Calvin Coolidge became president, he and his family hadn't yet moved into the White House. They were staying just two blocks away at one of Washington, D.C.'s most famous hotels.

Early one morning, the president was awakened from his sleep by a noise. He then saw a burglar going through his clothes, taking a wallet and a watch.

"I wish you wouldn't take that," he calmly said to the thief. Mr. Coolidge then told him that he was the president of the United States.

He convinced the burglar to put back the items that he had taken, and then they began to talk. The burglar was actually a college student who had run out of money while visiting Washington, D.C. He was unable to pay his hotel bill or to buy a train ticket back to his college.

Then the president reached into his wallet and gave the young man $32 but told him that it was only a loan and that he must pay it back. Before he left, President Coolidge also gave him some words of advice: "Son, you're a nice boy. You are better than you are acting. You are starting down the wrong road. Just remember who you are."

Sometime later, President Coolidge received a letter at the White House from the young man whom he had forgiven. In it was $32. He had repaid every cent of the loan that he had received from the nation's leader.

There are times when a good person does something bad, and before they can fix the problem, they end up making things worse. The young

President Calvin Coolidge

man was lucky that the person who he had tried to rob was President Calvin Coolidge, who gave him the best advice he could have ever received.

TODAY'S QUESTIONS

1. Who went into President Coolidge's room without permission?
2. How much money did President Coolidge give the young man?
3. When the young man sent President Coolidge a letter, what was in it?

President Herbert Hoover

CHAPTER 30

Herbert Hoover
The 31st President
1929–1933
It's the Herbert Hoover Show

Does your family own a television? If so, can you answer this: who was the first person ever to appear on television in the United States? Here's a hint: it wasn't an actor, an actress, or a cartoon character.

On April 7, 1927, a small group of people were invited to an auditorium in New York City to watch the first American test of a new invention called the television. It was a box that would send a live picture and voice sounds over telephone lines from Washington, D.C., to New York City.

That first broadcast wasn't a show as we know it today. It was the secretary of commerce, Herbert Hoover, who said, "I am glad to welcome television as the latest product of scientific discovery."

The testing was a success even though it would be another twenty years before people could begin buying their own sets. As for the man who first appeared on television, one year later (1928) he was elected president of the United States.

After he had retired from the White House, the former president wasn't that thrilled about television. Whenever he did watch, it was usually to view a baseball game.

But there was an interesting story from Mr. Hoover's days as president. Whenever he wanted to keep something secret from visitors, he and his wife would speak to each other in Chinese. From 1899 to 1901, the couple had lived in China, where they learned the language.

1. Who was the first person to appear on American television?
2. What happened to Mr. Hoover the year after he was on television?
3. Where did the Hoovers live from 1899 to 1901?

CHAPTER 31

Franklin D. Roosevelt
The 32nd President
1933–1945
Simple Is Better

Most leaders of a nation, like the president of the United States, have it pretty good. They live in a mansion; have someone drive them around in a big car; eat fancy food; and get paid a lot of money. That all sounds like fun, but sometimes the things in life that are simple are better.

An example of that took place in June 1939 when the king and queen of England visited America. It was the first time in history that the heads of the British royal family had ever come to the United States. It was up to President Franklin Roosevelt and his wife Eleanor to make sure that they had a good time.

The couple spent two days in Washington, D.C., where they saw the sights of the city and were the guests of a large parade through the streets. They were also honored at a large, formal White House dinner. After that, the president took the royal couple to his home in the countryside of Hyde Park, New York.

Even though President Roosevelt owned a mansion, its location was much more quiet and peaceful than Washington, D.C. During their visit, the Roosevelts took the king and queen on a picnic near their home, but they didn't serve them the fancy food that was cooked at the White House. For the picnic, the president served one of his favorite meals—hot dogs!

His mother Sara was shocked that the president would offer such common food to the king and queen of England. However, they had never had a hot dog, and as they ate their American picnic lunch, it was clear that they liked them. In fact, the king enjoyed his so much that he asked for a second one!

President Franklin D. Roosevelt

We often think that people expect to be treated like royalty, but sometimes in the end, it's best to keep things simple.

TODAY'S QUESTIONS

1. What was the home country of the king and queen?
2. Where was President Roosevelt's home?
3. What did President Roosevelt serve the king and queen for lunch at their picnic?

CHAPTER 32

Harry Truman
The 33rd President
1945–1953
The Piano and the President

Have you begun to think about what you might want to do when you grow up? Many young people have, while others are still making up their mind.

When Harry Truman was a boy, he knew what he wanted. It was to be a great pianist who would play with an orchestra. As a youngster, Harry would get up at five o'clock in the morning so that he could practice for two hours before leaving for school.

When he was fifteen years old, Harry attended a concert in Kansas City, Missouri, where he met one of his favorite pianists, Jan Pederewski from Poland. Although he loved the piano, he later realized that he just wasn't good enough to play with a great orchestra. After that, he went to work on his father's farm and in 1917 was sent to Europe to fight in World War I.

When he returned from the war, he ran a clothing store in Kansas City before starting a new career in politics. He served in many offices, and in 1945, he became the president of the United States even though he still enjoyed playing the piano. He would often play for his daughter Margaret, who was a professional singer, while she practiced.

Harry Truman's term as president ended in 1953. But in 1961, President Kennedy invited him back to Washington, D.C., giving a dinner in his honor. During that evening, the guests gathered in the East Room of the White House to listen to former president Harry Truman do the thing that he had always loved—play the piano.

Harry Truman's life took a different turn than what he had planned as a young person, but in the end he was a success. If you have a dream, remember what President Truman once said: "Believe and you're halfway there."

President Harry Truman performing on the piano at the White House in 1961

TODAY'S QUESTIONS

1. What was the musical instrument played by President Truman?
2. What time did President Truman get up in the morning to practice?
3. What was the other job that President Truman worked at after returning home from the war?

CHAPTER 33

Dwight D. Eisenhower
The 34th President
1953–1961
Dinner with the President

Do you enjoy food that has been barbecued? Each day, millions of Americans eat their barbecued meals at home or at a restaurant. Sometimes one of those people is the nation's leader.

Like other presidents, before he moved into the White House, Dwight Eisenhower had been a successful military leader. He had been the winning general of World War II.

But he also enjoyed doing something that many other people do at home. The president enjoyed barbecuing meat. It was not unusual to see President Eisenhower grilling steaks or chicken. But the place where he did the cooking was rather different.

Whenever the president wanted to get out of his office for a while and decided that he was in the mood to barbecue, he did so on top of the roof of the White House. He would go upstairs and exit onto the top level next to the Sun Room along with his Secret Service agents. It was there that he would cook for his family and be able to see all of the city of Washington, D.C.

By the way, like most of the famous barbecue chefs who are on television today, President Eisenhower would make his own barbecue sauce, which he would serve to his guests.

When President Eisenhower retired to his farm in Gettysburg, Pennsylvania, in 1961, he continued to barbecue meals, but not on the roof of the house. He built a patio for cooking.

President Dwight D. Eisenhower

1. Where did President Eisenhower barbecue his food?
2. What group was with the president while he was barbecuing?
3. What was the other item that President Eisenhower made for meals?

President John F. Kennedy

CHAPTER 34

John F. Kennedy
The 35th President
1961–1963
A True Hero

When a person is elected president of the United States, they often become a hero to many people. But that wasn't the case with John F. Kennedy, because he had been a true hero long before he moved into the White House.

During World War II, Mr. Kennedy was the skipper of a patrol torpedo boat known as *PT-109*. These were small crafts that could carry as many as eight torpedoes, which they used to sink the enemy's ships and submarines.

In the early morning of August 2, 1943, while on patrol in the Solomon Islands, *PT-109* was struck by a much larger Japanese destroyer. It hit the smaller vessel with such force that it sliced it in half, and two members of the crew lost their lives. As a fire raged, Lieutenant Kennedy gave the order to abandon ship, and his eleven remaining sailors dove into the water. After the fire was out, the crew climbed back onto the part of *PT-109* that was still afloat.

Fearing that they might be captured if they remained on the piece of the boat, Lieutenant Kennedy pointed toward a small area of land about four miles away known as Plum Pudding Island. He told his men, "We've got to swim to that."

They began swimming at 1:30 a.m. and finally arrived on the island five hours later. Lieutenant Kennedy had been a member of his college's swimming team and towed one of his wounded men the entire way using the strap of his life jacket.

They remained on Plum Pudding Island for several days until the coconuts—their only source of food—began to run low. At that point, they swam to another island. It was there that they were found by two friendly natives who worked for the New Zealand military. The eleven survivors were finally rescued six days after *PT-109* was sunk.

In 1944, Lieutenant Kennedy was presented the Navy Marine Corps Medal and the Purple Heart for his acts of courage. When someone would ask him how it felt to be a war hero, he would joke, "It was easy—*they sank my boat.*"

In 1960, the war hero was elected president of the United States. There is no greater act of courage than to risk your own life to save another. President Kennedy was an example of that type of courage.

TODAY'S QUESTIONS

1. What was the name of Lieutenant Kennedy's boat?
2. What was the name of the island the men swam toward?
3. How many days did it take to rescue the crew?

CHAPTER 35

Lyndon B. Johnson
The 36th President
1963–1969
The Joker Strikes Again

Do you enjoy playing jokes on your friends? Many people do, and that's O.K. as long as nobody gets hurt.

Once upon a time, we had a president who loved to play jokes on his friends, and he had a special car to help him do that. His name was Lyndon Johnson.

President Johnson was from Texas, where he owned a large ranch with horses, cattle, and a lake. He also owned an amphicar (am-feh-car).

By now you might be asking, "What is an amphicar?"

It's a special kind of car that was made in Germany, where a person can either drive on land like a regular car or in the water like a boat. It does float and won't sink.

One of the president's favorite pranks was to take guests for a ride around his ranch in his amphicar, but he wouldn't tell them that it worked in the water. Suddenly he would begin to drive toward his lake while yelling at his guests that he had lost control of the car as they headed toward the water. Once they went into the lake and the car stayed afloat, they realized that they had been tricked, as the president would begin laughing loudly while he steered the little car across the water.

President Johnson had fun with his amphicar, but he always made sure that no one got hurt.

President Lyndon Johnson takes some guests for a ride in his Amphicar.

TODAY'S QUESTIONS

1. What was the name of the car that President Johnson owned?
2. Where was President Johnson's ranch?
3. Where was the amphicar made?

CHAPTER 36

Richard Nixon
The 37th President
1969–1974
Try, Try Again

By now , you know that a person or a group doesn't win every time. As an example, think about your favorite sports team. Sometimes they win, but then again, sometimes they lose.

The same goes for almost every U.S. president who has lost at least one election before winning the race for the White House. One of those who lost his share of elections was Richard Nixon.

He started out by growing up in a poor family in California. As a boy, there were many times that he had to do without because the Nixons had no money. As he went through school, he became interested in running as a candidate in the campus elections.

In 1929, he ran for student-body president at his high school—he lost.

In 1960, he ran for president of the United States—he lost again.

In 1962, he ran for governor of California—he lost and was so discouraged that he said that he would never run for office again.

But a few years later, he met a group of people who gave him some advice about changes that he should make in his campaign. Mr. Nixon listened to their suggestions and made those changes.

In 1968, he ran for president and won. Four years later, he ran for re-election and won again. Mr. Nixon became the first president to visit all fifty states while in office and the first to visit Russia and China.

Like President Nixon found out, sometimes the difference between winning and losing is listening to advice from the right people, or as Thomas H. Palmer said in 1840, "If at first you don't succeed—try, try, try again."

President Richard Nixon

TODAY'S QUESTIONS

1. Where did President Nixon grow up?
2. What happened when he ran for president in 1960?
3. What happened to Mr. Nixon in 1968 after he listened to the advice?

CHAPTER 37

Gerald Ford

The 38th President

1974–1977

Always Be a Good Sport

Do you have a favorite football team? If so, who is your favorite player?

The University of Michigan has a history of very good football teams and players. In 1934, their Most Valuable Player was the team's center, Gerald Ford. He was good enough that some professional teams wanted him to play for them after he finished college.

But the players of the 1930s didn't make lots of money like they do today. So instead of playing pro football, he became a lawyer and then served in the Navy during World War II. He earned two Bronze Stars, which is one of the top medals presented by the U.S. military for being a hero.

In 1949, Mr. Ford was elected to Congress. In 1974, he became the president of the United States.

Mr. Ford was sixty-one years old when he took over as president. By that time, he was much too old to be playing football, but like many of our presidents, there was another sport that he enjoyed. That sport was golf.

However, like a lot of people, even though he liked golf, he wasn't very good at it. In 1974, he was playing in an event for charity in Minnesota when one of his shots struck a seventeen-year-old fan on the head. A few rounds later, he hit a golf cart that was carrying a policeman. In both cases, nobody was hurt.

Over the years, there were several other times when he would hit a ball and it would land in a crowd of people. In 1978, he was playing in California near the coast and hit one into the ocean, where it disappeared.

Even though the comics on television would often joke about President Ford's bad golfing, he never got mad and was always a good sport. In

97

President Gerald Ford practicing his golf swing on the White House lawn

fact, he kept on playing for many years after he retired because he liked the game. President Ford showed Americans that you don't have to be good at something to enjoy it. So if you enjoy something . . . just do it!

TODAY'S QUESTIONS

1. What sport did Gerald Ford play in college?
2. In World War II, was Gerald Ford in the Army or the Navy?
3. What sport did Gerald Ford enjoy playing while he was president?

CHAPTER 38

Jimmy Carter
The 39th President
1977–1981
The President and the Swamp Rabbit

When Jimmy Carter was president, one of his favorite ways to relax was to go fishing. His favorite places were in his home state of Georgia.

But in April 1979, President Carter came under attack while he was fishing. A creature came swimming toward his boat and tried to climb into it. The animal then made some hissing sounds.

President Carter said, "He jumped in the water and swam toward my boat. When he got almost there, I splashed some water with a paddle."

He swam off and was never seen again.

So who or what attacked the president of the United States back in 1979? No, it wasn't men from Mars.

It was a critter known as a swamp rabbit. It's a large cottontail that lives in swamps and can swim and run very fast.

It just goes to show that even the president has to be careful at all times.

TODAY'S QUESTIONS

1. In what state was President Carter fishing? Was it Texas or Georgia?
2. What type of animal attacked President Carter's boat?
3. What did President Carter use to drive the swamp rabbit away?

President Jimmy Carter

CHAPTER 39

Ronald Reagan

The 40th President

1981–1989

The President's Co-Star

Have you ever dreamed of being a well-known actor? We once had a president who had done just that.

Ronald Reagan was the only person to have been a professional actor before he became president. In fact from 1937 to 1965, he made sixty-nine movies and appeared in a number of television programs.

Many of Mr. Reagan's acting roles had him playing cowboys or soldiers. He also co-starred with some of the most beautiful actresses of that era.

But one of his most successful movies wasn't an action thriller, and his co-star was quite different from any that he had in his other films. In 1951, Mr. Reagan made a comedy called *Bedtime for Bonzo*. Bonzo was his co-star, and he was a chimpanzee!

The movie was a hit among the public, although Mr. Reagan didn't care much for acting with a chimp even if it did give his movie career a boost. He said that he didn't watch the film until 1984 while he was president. The movie is still popular today among those who rent videos.

Ronald Reagan proved that as an actor or as president, sometimes you have to do things that you may not want to do even though they often work out for the best.

TODAY'S QUESTIONS

1. What type of work did Ronald Reagan do before he was president?
2. Who was Bonzo?
3. Did the public like *Bedtime for Bonzo*?

Future president Ronald Reagan in 1951 with his co-star Bonzo

CHAPTER 40

George H. W. Bush
The 41st President
1989–1993
The Family Tree

There are people who are curious about the history of their family. Many of them will study records to get answers about their long-lost relatives, known as ancestors. This type of study is called genealogy.

Many of the presidents know about the past of their family members. Some are not special, while others are related to some well-known people from history. One former president can boast about some pretty famous ancestors in his background.

You have probably heard about the Pilgrims. They were a group of settlers from England who were looking for a new land where they could freely live and worship their religion. In 1620, they boarded a ship named the *Mayflower*, which crossed the Atlantic Ocean before docking at Plymouth, Massachusetts. They settled there and built a colony.

The Pilgrims have become famous for starting the tradition known as Thanksgiving. It was a feast to give thanks for all of the good things that had happened to them.

In 1988, George H. W. Bush was elected president of the United States. His ancestors include John Howland, Francis Cooke, and John Tilley, who were all members of the Pilgrims. Also, President Bush's wife Barbara is related to another Pilgrim, Henry Samson.

No doubt that Thanksgiving is a special time when the Bush family gets together.

President George H. W. Bush

TODAY'S QUESTIONS

1. What is the name of the group in which the Bush family has ancestors?
2. Where did the Pilgrims arrive in 1620?
3. What is the holiday that began with the Pilgrims?

CHAPTER 41

Bill Clinton
The 42nd President
1993–2001
The Music Man

There have been a number of presidents who have played musical instruments. For example, Thomas Jefferson, John Tyler, and Abraham Lincoln each played the violin, while Franklin Roosevelt, Harry Truman, and Richard Nixon made music on the piano. But only one president played the saxophone, and that was Bill Clinton.

He had a talent for music, taking part as a member of the chorus and playing the tenor saxophone at Hot Springs High School. Mr. Clinton won first chair in the Arkansas state band's saxophone section and played in the marching band during football games at Hot Springs High School. Each summer, he attended a band camp in the Ozark Mountains.

At one point in his life, he considered becoming a professional musician but decided to enter politics after meeting President Kennedy just before his senior year of high school. A few years later, he was elected governor of Arkansas, becoming the second youngest man to hold the office.

Mr. Clinton continued to practice music and used his talents as a saxophone player while campaigning for president. In 1992, he played the song "Heartbreak Hotel" on *The Arsenio Hall Show* as millions of viewers watched on television. Shortly after the performance, he went on to win the election.

In 2007, former president Clinton signed and donated the saxophone that he played at his inauguration to the American Jazz Museum in Kansas City, Missouri. If you have a talent in music, keep working at it, because good things could be coming your way.

President Bill Clinton

1. What is the instrument that President Clinton played?
2. What is President Clinton's home state?
3. Who was the president that Mr. Clinton met while he was in high school?

President George W. Bush

CHAPTER 42

George W. Bush
The 43rd President
2001–2009
What's in a Name?

There are many things that a person needs if they are going to become the president of the United States. One of them is a good memory, because on that job, there is a great deal to remember, like the names of the world's nations and their leaders.

People who know former president George W. Bush say that he has a photographic memory. Because of that, he is able to remember the names of large numbers of people along with other items.

In the 1960s when he was a student at Yale University, Mr. Bush belonged to a group called a fraternity, of which there were fifty-five members. He was the only one who could identify each of them by name. He also memorized the names of almost two thousand of his classmates listed in the student directory.

His ability to remember names and faces was helpful when he successfully ran for office, first as governor of Texas and then as president of the United States.

He was not only a master at recalling names, but could also memorize the statistics of players and teams of his favorite sport—baseball. Before he was president, from 1989 to 1998, Mr. Bush was a co-owner of the Texas Rangers baseball team. Today he lives in Dallas and can often be seen at a Rangers game.

TODAY'S QUESTIONS

1. What do many people call President Bush's type of memory?
2. Where did President Bush go to college?
3. Before he was president, Mr. Bush was governor of what state?

109

President Barack Obama

CHAPTER 43

Barack Obama
The 44th President
2009–2017
The Obama Collection

In 2009, Barack Obama became the first American president whose father had been born in Africa. His dad was from the country of Kenya.

Before he became a politician, Mr. Obama had been a lawyer, which requires a great deal of reading. But he wasn't just reading books about the law.

Like many people, Mr. Obama enjoyed collecting items. Many people choose to collect things like coins or stamps. Few people knew that before he became a candidate for president, Mr. Obama had a collection of other books. But not just any books. He has a large number of comic books. His favorites are *Spider-Man* and *Conan the Barbarian*.

Through the years, many comic book companies have featured President Obama as a character in their stories. His image has appeared in *Spider-Man*, *Savage Dragon*, and *Archie* comics among others.

In addition, President Obama has read every *Harry Potter* book in the series but said that his all-time favorite novel is *Moby Dick*, the classic story of a great white whale. However, he is not only an enthusiastic reader, he is also a successful writer. Before becoming president, Mr. Obama wrote two best-selling books about his life.

So when your homework is done, get a copy of one of your favorite books and just read.

TODAY'S QUESTIONS

1. Where was President Obama's father's home country?
2. What types of books does President Obama collect?
3. What is President Obama's favorite novel?

Answer Key for Chapter Questions

1—George Washington
  1.) Philadelphia
  2.) $150
  3.) American Revolution
2—John Adams
  1.) John Adams
  2.) The great castle
  3.) The Secret Service
3—Thomas Jefferson
  1.) Big Bone Lick, Kentucky
  2.) They sank on a riverboat that was traveling on the Mississippi River.
  3.) Fossil
4—James Madison
  1.) The First Lady
  2.) She created the "bombe glacée" dessert.
  3.) Oyster
5—James Monroe
  1.) England and France
  2.) George Washington
  3.) The White House
6—John Quincy Adams
  1.) Antoine Giusta
  2.) The boat sank.
  3.) They swam to shore.
7—Andrew Jackson
  1.) He held a public gathering at the White House.
  2.) Two hours
  3.) Thomas Jefferson
8—Martin Van Buren
  1.) Old Kinderhook
  2.) Things are good.
  3.) He lost.
9—William Henry Harrison
  1.) He studied to be a doctor.
  2.) He joined the military.
  3.) Because he made little money
10—John Tyler
  1.) Four years
  2.) A cannon exploded.
  3.) They wanted to keep the newspaper reporters away.

11—James K. Polk
  1.) That he would only serve one term
  2.) Yes
  3.) It will earn the respect of other people.
12—Zachary Taylor
  1.) He was a soldier.
  2.) Where a candidate appears at events before the voters
  3.) President Taylor's horse
13—Millard Fillmore
  1.) None
  2.) It was burned during a fire.
  3.) A line of people who passed buckets of water to one another to put out a fire
14—Franklin Pierce
  1.) George Washington
  2.) Franklin Pierce
  3.) She was not hurt.
15—James Buchanan
  1.) James Buchanan
  2.) A slave state
  3.) Pennsylvania
16—Abraham Lincoln
  1.) Wrestling
  2.) Illinois
  3.) Lawyer
17—Andrew Johnson
  1.) North Carolina
  2.) They make clothes.
  3.) A copy of the U.S. Constitution
18—Ulysses S. Grant
  1.) He was charged with speeding.
  2.) He was fishing out of season.
  3.) Benjamin Franklin
19—Rutherford B. Hayes
  1.) Something that continues to take place over many years
  2.) Congress passed a law that kids couldn't play on the Capitol grounds.
  3.) He invited them to play with their Easter eggs on the White House lawn.

20—James Garfield
  1.) It means that a person can write (or perform other tasks) with either hand.
  2.) Latin and Greek
  3.) German

21—Chester Arthur
  1.) New York City
  2.) Eighty
  3.) Taking walks in Washington, D.C.

22—Grover Cleveland
  1.) New York
  2.) "We'll be back."
  3.) To do what is right

23—Benjamin Harrison
  1.) President William Henry Harrison
  2.) Electric
  3.) They were afraid of being shocked.

24—William McKinley
  1.) A carriage
  2.) His coat
  3.) Ohio

25—Theodore Roosevelt
  1.) So that some animals would not become extinct
  2.) Yes
  3.) Yes

26—William Howard Taft
  1.) He wrote a personal note.
  2.) Turkeys
  3.) He signed his autograph to have it mailed to people who had requested it.

27—Woodrow Wilson
  1.) He had a learning difficulty.
  2.) George Washington
  3.) No

28—Warren Harding
  1.) Laddie Boy
  2.) Rin Tin Tin
  3.) Melted pennies

29—Calvin Coolidge
  1.) A burglar
  2.) $32
  3.) He repaid the $32.

30—Herbert Hoover
  1.) Herbert Hoover
  2.) He was elected president.
  3.) China

31—Franklin D. Roosevelt
  1.) England
  2.) Hyde Park, New York
  3.) Hot dogs

32—Harry Truman
  1.) The piano
  2.) 5:00 a.m.
  3.) He ran a clothing store.

33—Dwight D. Eisenhower
  1.) On the roof of the White House
  2.) The Secret Service
  3.) Barbecue sauce

34—John F. Kennedy
  1.) *PT-109*
  2.) Plum Pudding Island
  3.) Six days

35—Lyndon Johnson
  1.) The amphicar
  2.) Texas
  3.) Germany

36—Richard Nixon
  1.) California
  2.) He lost.
  3.) He was elected president.

37—Gerald Ford
  1.) Football
  2.) Navy
  3.) Golf

38—Jimmy Carter
  1.) Georgia
  2.) Swamp rabbit
  3.) The boat paddle

39—Ronald Reagan
  1.) He was an actor.
  2.) He was a chimpanzee who was in movies.
  3.) Yes

40—George H. W. Bush
  1.) The Pilgrims
  2.) Plymouth, Massachusetts
  3.) Thanksgiving

41—Bill Clinton
  1.) The saxophone
  2.) Arkansas
  3.) President Kennedy

42—George W. Bush
  1.) Photographic
  2.) Yale University
  3.) Texas

43—Barack Obama
  1.) Kenya
  2.) Comic books
  3.) *Moby Dick*

References

ARTICLES CONSULTED

Associated Press: "Coolidge Loaned Money to His Hotel-Room Thief" (*Lexington, N.C. Dispatch*; August 6, 1983).

audiegrl: "The History of Christmas at the White House (1901–1953)" (the 44-diaries; December 21, 2009).

Chestnut, J. LeCount: untitled article (*Washington Post*; November 7, 1925).

Cole, John Y.: "Fillmore's Foundation" (Library of Congress; July/August 2010).

Ferling, John: "George Washington: His Final Days" (history.net; December 1999).

Fleming, Thomas: "John F. Kennedy's PT-109 Disaster" (history.net; August 2, 2012).

Fuller, Jaime: "That Time FDR Served Hot Dogs to the King, and Three Other Strange State Dinner Facts" (*Washington Post*; February 11, 2014).

Graham, Bryan Arman: "Abraham Lincoln Was a Skilled Wrestler and World-Class Trash Talker" (*Sports Illustrated*; February 12, 2013).

Hainthaler, Joe: "5 Facts about James Buchanan" (Lancaster Newspaper, Inc.; February 17, 2014).

Huey, Rodney A.: "An Abbreviated History of the Circus in America" (circusfederation .org; retrieved August 26, 2014).

Jackson, Brooks: "Jimmy Carter Attacked by Killer Rabbit" (*Washington Post*; April 20, 1979).

Jewett, Thomas O.: "Thomas Jefferson Paleontologist" (*Early America Review*; Fall 2000).

Kelly, Kate: "Laddie Boy, Warren Harding's Dog" (americacomesalive.com; retrieved September 5, 2014).

Kristof, Nicholas D.: "Ally of an Older Generation Amid the Tumult of the 60s" (*New York Times*; June 19, 2000).

Onion, Rebecca: "When LBJ Drove on Water" (Slate.com; retrieved September 6, 2014).

Segraves, Mark: "D.C. Police Once Arrested a U.S. President for Speeding" (wtop.com; October 6, 2012).

Spamer, Earle E. and McCourt, Richard M.: "Lewis—*and* Clark—at Big Bone Lick" (lewis-clark.org; August 2006).

Staff Report: "Metro Policeman Arrests U.S. President for Speeding" (ghostsofdc.org; March 4, 2014).

Staff Report: "Tyler Narrowly Escapes Death on the USS Princeton" (history.com; retrieved September 10, 2014).

Swaine, Jon: "Barack Obama: The 50 Facts You Might Not Know" (*UK Telegraph*; November 7, 2008).

Tedeschi, Diane: "The White House's First Celebrity Dog" (Smithsonian.com; January 22, 2009).

Trex, Ethan: "Andrew Jackson's Big Block of Cheese" (*Mental Floss*; January 26, 2014).

BOOKS CONSULTED

Bedini, Silvio: *Thomas Jefferson and American Vertebrate Paleontology* (Virginia Division of Mineral Resources, Publication 61; 1985).

Bergeron, Paul H.: *Andrew Johnson* (*Tennessee Encyclopedia of History and Culture*; 2009).

Boeller, Paul F.: *Presidential Anecdotes* (Oxford University Press; 1996).

Calvin, William H.: *The Throwing Madonna: Essays on the Brain* (McGraw-Hill; 1983).

Clinton, Bill: *My Life* (Random House; 2004).

Dusinberre, William: *Slavemaster President: The Double Career of James Polk* (Oxford University Press; 2003).

Edge, Laura Bufano: *William McKinley* (Twenty-First Century Books; 2007).

Eliot, Marc: *Reagan: The Hollywood Years* (Crown Archetype; 2008).

Grosvenor Library: *Grosvenor Library Bulletin*, Volumes 3–4 (RareBooksClub.com; 2012).

Leish, Kenneth W.: *The White House: A History of the Presidents* (*Newsweek*; 1977).

Mansfield, Stephen: *The Faith of George W. Bush* (Tarcher; 2004).

Nevins, Allan: *The Diary of John Quincy Adams, 1794–1845* (Charles Scribner's Sons; 1951).

Scarry, Robert J.: *Millard Fillmore* (McFarland; 2010).

Seale, William: *The President's House* (White House Historical Association; 1986).

Trefousse, Hans L.: *Andrew Johnson: A Biography* (W. W. Norton & Company; Reissue edition; 1997).

Van Natta, Don: *First Off the Tee: Presidential Hackers, Duffers, and Cheaters from Taft to Bush* (PublicAffairs; 2003).

Wilmeth, Don B. and Bigsby, Christopher: *The Cambridge History of American Theatre* (Cambridge University Press; 2000).

WEBSITES CONSULTED

eyewitnesstohistory.com
history.com
mountvernon.org
potus.com
whitehouse.gov1.info
whitehousehistory.org

Acknowledgments

Dwight D. Eisenhower Presidential Library and Museum
Franklin D. Roosevelt Presidential Library and Museum
George Bush Presidential Library and Museum
Gerald R. Ford Presidential Library
Harry S. Truman Library and Museum
Herbert Hoover Presidential Library and Museum
John F. Kennedy Presidential Library and Museum
John F. Marszalek, the executive director of the Ulysses S. Grant Presiden-
  tial Collection at Mississippi State University
Lyndon Baines Johnson Library and Museum
National Park Service
Richard Nixon Presidential Library and Museum
Ronald Reagan Presidential Library and Center for Public Affairs

Photo Credits

pp. x, 38, 48, 49, 50, 56, 60, 66, 72, 74, 78, 84, 96, 100, 104, 106, 109, and 111: Library of Congress Prints and Photographs Division, Washington, DC 20540 USA

pp. 2, 6, 8, 10, 16, 22, 28, 30, and 40: Thinkstock

p. 14: Taken from a daguerreotype by P. Haas; lith. & publ. by P. Haas, Washington City. Library of Congress Prints and Photographs Division, Washington, DC 20540 USA

p. 20: From an original painting by H. Inman; lith. & publ. by P. Haas, Washington City. Library of Congress Prints and Photographs Division, Washington, DC 20540 USA

p. 24: From life on stone by Chs. Fenderich 1841. Library of Congress Prints and Photographs Division, Washington, DC 20540 USA

p. 34: Engraved by J. Sartain. Library of Congress Prints and Photographs Division, Washington, DC 20540 USA

p. 36: Designed and engraved on steel by W. L. Ormsby, NY Library of Congress Prints and Photographs Division, Washington, DC 20540 USA

p. 42: Printed in oil colors, by Bingham & Dod, Hartford, CT. Library of Congress Prints and Photographs Division, Washington, DC 20540 USA

p. 44: C. Schussele 1863; eng. By William Sartain, Philadelphia. Library of Congress Prints and Photographs Division, Washington, DC 20540 USA

p. 54: Lith. By Buek & Lindner, 65 Warren St., NY. Library of Congress Prints and Photographs Division, Washington, DC 20540 USA

p. 68: National Park Service (public domain)

p. 80: Courtesy of AT&T Archives and History Center

p. 86: John J. Kennedy Library

p. 88: Fabian Bachrach, Library of Congress Prints and Photographs Division, Washington, DC 20540 USA

p. 90: Photograph by Frank Turgeon Jr. in the John F. Kennedy Presidential Library and Museum, Boston (public domain)

p. 94: LBJ Library photo by Yoichi Okamoto (public domain)

p. 98: Photo by David Hume Kennerly, courtesy Gerald R. Ford Library (public domain)

p. 102: The Everett Collection

About the Author

For thirty-one years, **Mike Henry** taught American history to students at all levels of the educational spectrum from elementary school to college. His technique of using the events of the past to show how they impact our lives in the present made him a popular classroom instructor and guest speaker. From the inception of the No Child Left Behind Act, he averaged a success rate of more than 80 percent on state-mandated testing where a majority of his students were considered to be at the poverty level.

Mike is a two-time recipient of the nationally recognized award Who's Who Among America's Classroom Teachers.

His interest in American history comes naturally, as his ancestors fought in battles against the redcoats in South Carolina during the American Revolution. A couple of centuries later, Mike became the first member of his family to attain both undergraduate and graduate degrees.

In 1994, he published his first work, a historical novel entitled *Peacemaker: The Saga of an American Family*. The author retired from the classroom in 2008.

Mike and his wife Pamela, who is also a retired educator, reside near Dallas, Texas.